4 4 2

442

PUBLISHED BY LITTLE NALU PICTURES, LLC
FIRST PRINT EDITION, 2018   ISBN: 978-0-692-15676-6

STELA

ORIGINALLY PUBLISHED ON STELA UNLIMITED APP (AVAILABLE ON IOS/ ANDROID)
© 2016 BY BREAKOUTBIT INTERNATIONAL, INC.

EDITED BY RYAN YOUNT

THE CREATORS OF 442 WOULD LIKE TO DEDICATE THIS TO ALL THE NISEI WORLD WAR II VETERANS WHO FOUGHT AND OFTEN SACRIFICED THEIR LIVES SO WE CAN BE FREE.

ROB WOULD LIKE TO DEDICATE 442 TO HIS GRANDFATHER, S. SGT. ROY H. SATO, AND THE SATO FAMILY.

KOJI WOULD LIKE TO DEDICATE 442 TO HIS SON SO THAT HE LIVES HIS LIFE IN THE GO FOR BROKE SPIRIT.

PHINNEAS WOULD LIKE TO DEDICATE 442 TO HIS FATHER, KRIS, HIS FAMILY, AND ALL THOSE WHO STRUGGLED TO BETTER THIS COUNTRY.

SPECIAL THANKS GO TO
THE CALIFORNIA STATE LIBRARY, ERIC NAKAMURA & GIANT ROBOT, GO FOR BROKE NATIONAL EDUCATION CENTER, JAPANESE AMERICAN NATIONAL MUSEUM, VISUAL COMMUNICATIONS

4 4 2

WRITTEN BY KOJI STEVEN SAKAI & PHINNEAS KIYOMURA

ILLUSTRATED BY ROB SATO

LITTLE NALU PICTURES, LLC
LOS ANGELES, CALIFORNIA

CHAPTER 1

On February 19, 1942, two months after the bombing of Pearl Harbor by Japan, 120,000 Japanese Americans were forced to leave their homes and relocate to remote prison camps. Their only crime? Looking like the enemy.

Two years later, the 442nd Regimental Combat Team, a segregated fighting unit primarily composed of Japanese Americans, were fighting in Europe—this despite the fact that many of their families were still in the camps. These men would go on to become the most highly decorated fighting force of its size and duration in United States Army history.

This is their story...

MANZANAR WAR RELOCATION CENTER, CALIFORNIA, 1943

CHAPTER 2

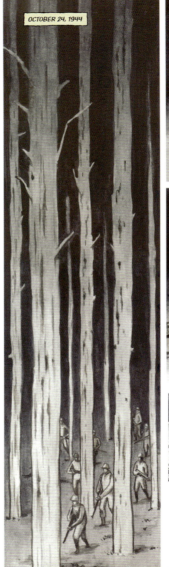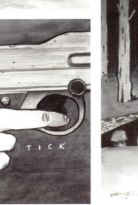

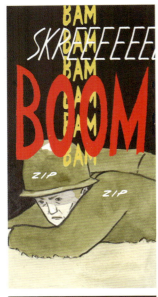

CHAPTER

CHAPTER 4

CHAPTER

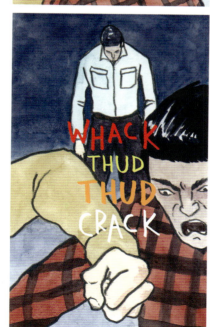

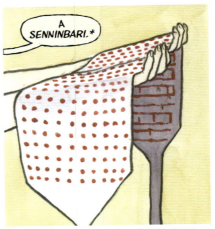

CHAPTER 6

CHAPTER 7

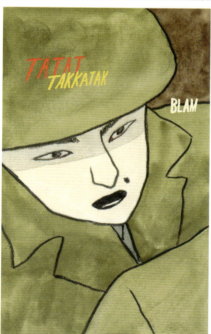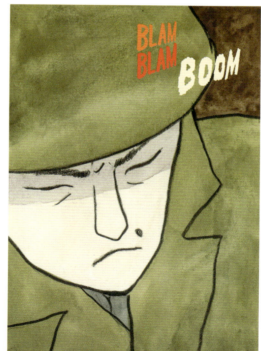

CHAPTER 8

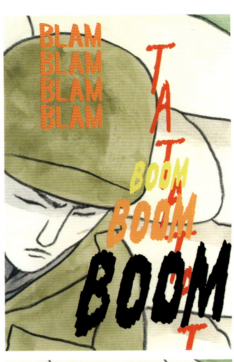

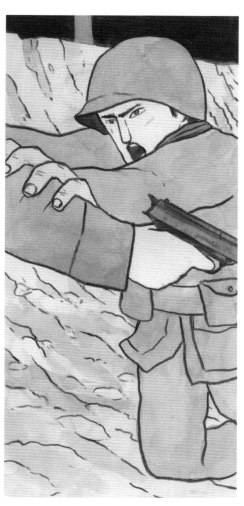

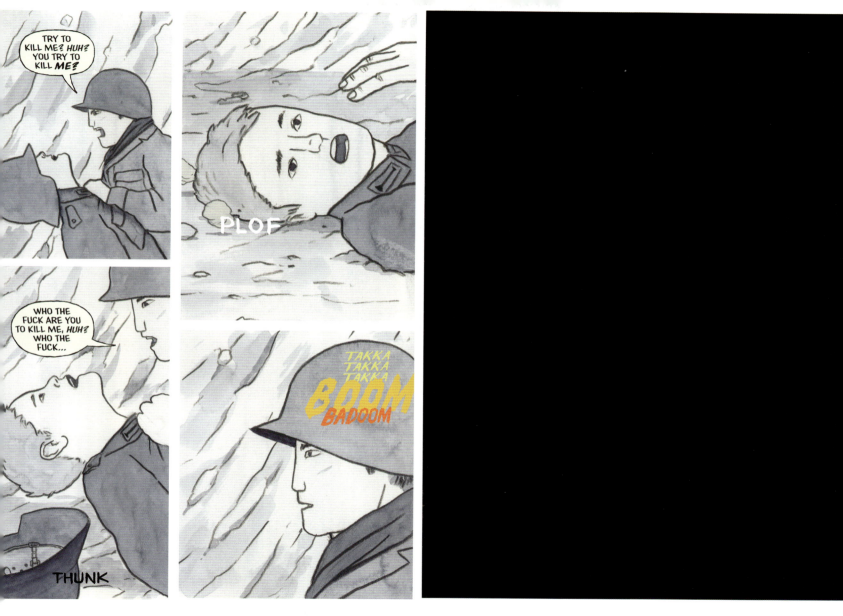

CHAPTER 9

CHAPTER 10

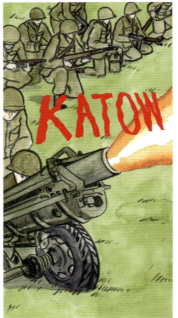

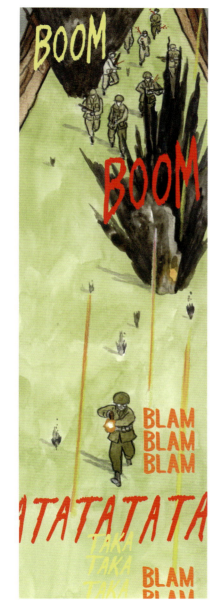

CHAPTER 11

CHAPTER 12

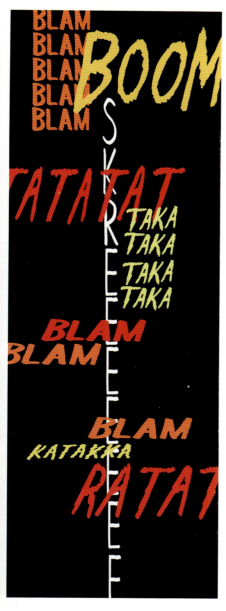